Wonders

Program Authors

Diane August
Donald R. Bear
Janice A. Dole
Jana Echevarria
Douglas Fisher
David Francis
Vicki Gibson

Jan Hasbrouck
Margaret Kilgo
Jay McTighe
Scott G. Paris
Timothy Shanahan
Josefina V. Tinajero

Mc
Graw
Hill
Education

Cover and Title pages: Nathan Love

www.mheonline.com/readingwonders

Send all inquiries to:
McGraw-Hill Education
2 Penn Plaza
New York, NY 10121

ISBN: 978-0-07-678430-1
MHID: 0-07-678430-4

Printed in the United States of America.

2 3 4 5 6 7 8 9 RMN 20 19 18 17 16

A

Unit 7 The Animal Kingdom

The Big Idea: What are different kinds of animals?

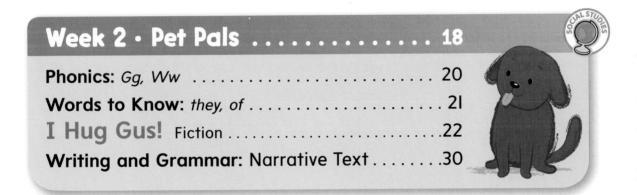

(t) WorldFoto/Alamy; (c) Amy Cartwright; (b) Edit Sliacka

Essential Question

How are some animals alike and how are they different?

Go Digital!

COLLABORATE

Talk About It

How is a kitten like a duckling?
How is it different?

Image Source/Corbis

4

Amazing Animals

Uu

Say the name of each picture.

1

2

Read each word.

3 **us**   **mud**   **fun**

4 **rub**   **hum**   **tuck**

for   have

He can run **for** a long time.

Elephants **have** big ears.

7

A Pup
and a Cub

I am a pup.
I **have** a mom and a dad.

Arco Images/GmbH/Alamy

I am in a pack.
We sit in a den.

I am not a pet.
I have not met a pet pup!

11

I am a cub.

Mom and Dad see me.

I sit on a rock in the sun.
I nap in the sun a lot!

Sis and I have fun.
We can go up, up!

A pup can run **for** fun.
A cub can run **for** fun.

A Pup and a Cub

Pages 8–15

Write About the Text

Steve

I answered the question: **How do the wolf pup and the lion cub feel around their families?**

Student Model: *Informative Text*

Details

I used details in the photos to figure out how the pup feels.

The wolf pup feels safe with the family.

The family lives in a den.

The wolf pup feels happy around its family.

3sbworld/iStock/Getty Images Plus/Getty Images

16

Specific Words
I used the word
safe to tell how the
lion cub feels.

The lion cub feels safe with
its family.
The cub stays close to
its family.
It also feels safe enough
to climb with Sis.

Grammar
Climb tells
what the
cub does.
Climb is a
verb.

COLLABORATE

Your Turn

How are the wolf
pup and the lion
cub the same? How
are they different?

Go Digital!
Write your response online.
Use your editing checklist.

17

Essential Question
How do you take care of different kinds of pets?

Go Digital!

Animal Pals

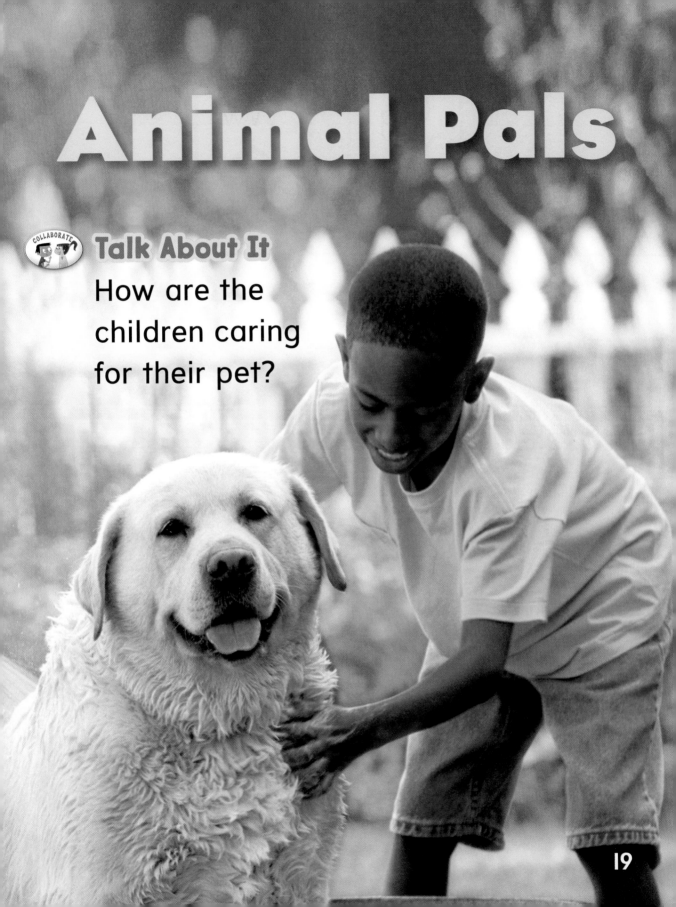

Talk About It

How are the children caring for their pet?

19

Say the name of each picture.

1

2

Read each word.

3 hug   get   tag

4 wet   win   wag

they

of

They went to the park.

I take care **of** my fish.

21

I Hug Gus!

I can see a big, red pup.
I pick a pup for a pet.

23

My big pup and a cat tug.
They tug and have fun.

Gus is a big, red pup.
Gus can run, run, and win!

Amy Cartwright

Gus is on top **of** the bed.
He can sit up and beg.

Gus and I are on a rug.
Gus can tug, tug, tug!

I rub Gus in the tub.
Gus is wet, wet, wet!

Amy Cartwright

I tuck Gus in a big bed.
I can hug, hug, hug Gus!

Amy Cartwright

I Hug Gus!

Pages 22–29

Write About the Text

Lucas

I responded to the prompt: **Write about getting a new pet. Use the word I and tell what happened.**

Student Model: *Narrative Text*

One day, my Mom and I went to the park. We saw a lost parrot on the bench. We rescued it! I felt happy!

Reaction
I reacted to an event like the boy in the story.

**Describing
Words**
I used the
word **lost**
to describe
the parrot.

Mom and I put up signs.

No one claimed the lost bird.

So, we kept him.

We found him in Carl
Schurz Park.

That's why we named
him Carl!

Grammar

Kept is a
verb.

COLLABORATE

Your Turn

Narrate a story
about the first day
with a new pet.

Go Digital!
Write your response online.
Use your editing checklist.

Essential Question

Where do animals live?

Go Digital!

Home, Sweet Home!

Talk About It

Where does this animal live?

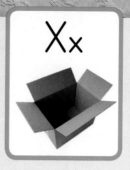

Say the name of each picture.

1

2

Read each word.

3 vet   vat   van

4 mix   wax   fix

said

want

Read Together

The vet said Max is fine.

I want to see a box.

A Vet in a Van

I am a vet in a van.
I **want** to see a red fox.

37

"I am a red fox," **said** a fox.
"A fox can sit in a den."

Edit Sliacka

I want to see a big cat.
I can go in my van.

39

"I am a big cat," said a cat.
"I can sit on a rock."

Edit Sliacka

I can see a pig.
I can see six!

Edit Sliacka

I see a sick ox.
I can fix a bad leg.

"I met a vet!" said the ox.
"A vet can fix a sick ox!"

43

Edit Sliacka

A Vet in a Van

Pages 36–43

Write About the Text

Kelly

I responded to the prompt: **Write a book report about which animals you liked best in "A Vet in a Van."**

Student Model: *Opinion*

Details
I used picture details to help me form my opinion.

I liked the fox and the ox best in the story.
I liked the fox because of his sly look.

Grammar

The word **liked** is a **verb.**

I liked the ox.

He was willing to be helped.

He looked cute with the bandage on.

I liked the fox and the ox because they both are brave.

My Feelings

I wrote my opinion about a fox and an ox.

Your Turn

COLLABORATE

Write a book report about your opinion about the art in the story.

Go Digital!
Write your response online.
Use your editing checklist.